P9-DBY-610

Books by Marie Ponsot

THE
GREEN DARK

THE
GREEN DARK

POEMS BY
MARIE PONSOT

ALFRED A. KNOPF NEW YORK 1988

THIS IS A BORZOI BOOK
PUBLISHED BY ALFRED A. KNOPF, INC.

"Outside the Fertile Crescent" was originally published
in *City Lights Review*.

"De-fusing the Usual Criminal Metaphors" was
originally published in *Commonweal*.

"Museum Out Of Mind" was originally published in *13th Moon*.

"Take Time, Take Place," "On a Library of Congress photo
of Eunice B. Winkless, 1904," and "Myopia Makes All
Light Sources Radiant" were originally published in *Open Places*.

Library of Congress Cataloging-in-Publication Data

Ponsot, Marie.
   The green dark.

   I. Title.
PS3531.049G674 1988   811'.54   87–46186
ISBN 0–394–57054–5

Manufactured in the United States of America
First Edition

I gratefully acknowledge the gifts
of time and places from
the MACDOWELL COLONY
the FONDATION KAROLYI
and the NATIONAL ENDOWMENT FOR THE ARTS

and dedicate this collection of poems
to ROSEMARY & LEONARD DEEN,
"sublime energizers"

CONTENTS

vii

TAKE TIME, TAKE PLACE

THE
GREEN DARK

ON A LIBRARY OF CONGRESS PHOTO
OF EUNICE B. WINKLESS, 1904

Eunice, flexible flyer of summer, rides
across the noon fair
short-stirruped astride
her tall white mare,
her power implied
loosely in a practised grip.
Her life is in her hands;
her living found, she lets nothing slip.

The pool glints like a tame star on the ground.
The ramp up the two-story tower, if
ramshackle, is ready.
Martial music starts.
Here she comes bareback. Having hitched
her triple-flounced Gibson-girl arts lightly
about her, her hands rein calm in.

Regal as Iphigenia
taking the upward course
in a drift of white eyelet muslin
she rides the animal horse.
Merrily fife & drum pace
their climb. Women think prayers,
set to not-look, just in case.
Men do not snigger, forget
their faces/ladies/bets, and stare
once she reaches the platform.
Music quits her exalted there.
Sounds, gathered to silence, swarm
stormhead about her stance. This crowd, knowing

horses, wonders if the big mare
shudders as it holds still. The pool shows
flatness: no wind. That's good. A brittle
drumroll rains. The drumsticks stop.
She leans to the mare's neck, smiling a little.

Out & groundless horse & girl drop
flying clear of equilibrium
Her body jockeying air
touches only bridle & with one
knee, horse, as nothing to spare
they head for the hope they head
in dread in dread for the pool.

To herself she says among her wet hair,
"Did it again. Damn fool."

I need her dreadful ease, its immense self-reference.
I watch to catch her hand-span skill address
the radius of her practise then guess,
self-tested, at its circumference.

Yet since I made all this up from one snapshot
it is fictive ink, not history.
What I think of her may be ready or not
to be telling. Who can make sense?

And, when do I act on better evidence?

THE STORY
OF THE PROBLEMS

THE PROBLEM OF FREEDOM
& COMMITMENT

In her first dot-to-dot book of puzzles
the last one left undone looks too hard.
It has hundreds of numbers. She prefers
the two-digit ones that trace out as
big-headed animals with big eyes
but she decides to give this one a try.
Soon she has a notion of one part of how
the picture will turn out to be.
She doesn't like it. Not one bit. She sees
it may be more trouble than it's worth so she goes
slower, hunting for the next consecutive
numbers, no longer anxious to find them
but anxious once they're found, fixed on,
and another strand of line goes down.
"It's too much. It's all mixed up," she thinks.
"Even the good parts are scribbly. There are
millions of books like this, all different;
I could just leave this mess and get
a new book, with no horrors in it,
a nice one, that I'd like." But she goes on
absent-minded, thinking *picture*, working out
the one she's started, worse and worse.
Right now there's nothing else to do, and if, she thinks,
she's false to this the first unpleasant one,
which is so complex her predictions are guesses,
which could be the most important one in the book,
maybe no puzzle will make her take a second look
and nothing she starts on will ever get done.

THE PROBLEM OF SOCIAL GROWTH

From an enthroned woman to whom she brings
her careful grab at dangle of brass ring
she accepts a nod as victory.
Large hand to small, a ticket has conveyed
that they are two graces whose smiles agree.
A winner, she blushes at accolade,
thinks she shd offer Crackerjacks
but can't. The ticket is green, torn short.
She finds the starter man and gives it back,
the token of power, her first earned passport
to a discus world a woman oversees.
She finds her best outside horse, climbs astride,
and spins Olympic on the victory's
round momentum that grown-ups, she thinks, ride.

THE PROBLEM OF THE
EXPERIMENTAL METHOD

Today she learns that up is marvelous.
Water rises up unseen, falls, and appears
as crystals, their difference too sharp for us
to see without a magnifying glass,
or save, or savor. She feels ridiculous
(a scrap of velvet on her glove, a mass
of squashed snow underfoot) trying to dry
the lens, land a flake on velvet, and look.
It's not necessary. She feels like a spy.
She'd rather find snow pictures in her book
and read (and agree) about earth's atmosphere.
Cold. Experiments don't take her far.
Words do, without policing. Words keep here, here.
Their gravity homes her, on her native star.

THE PROBLEM OF FICTION

She always writes poems. This summer
she's starting a novel. It's in trouble already.
The characters are easy—a girl
and her friend who is a girl
and the boy down the block with his first car,
an older boy, sixteen, who sometimes
these warm evenings leaves his house to go dancing
in dressy clothes though it's still light out.
The girl has a brother who has lots of friends,
is good in math, and just plain good which
doesn't help the story. The story
should have rescues & escapes in it
which means who's the bad guy; he couldn't be
the brother or the grandpa or the father either,
or even the boy down the block with his first car.
People in novels have to need something,
she thinks, that it takes about
two hundred pages to get.
She can't imagine that. Nothing
she needs can be got; if it could
she'd go get it: the answer to nightmares;
a mother who'd be proud of her; doing things
a mother could be proud of; having hips
& knowing how to squeal at the beach laughing
when the boy down the block picked her up & carried her
& threw her in the water. If she'd laughed
squealing he might still take her swimming
& his mother wouldn't say she's crazy, she would
not have got her teeth into his shoulder till
well yes she bit him, and the marks

lasted & lasted, his mother said so,
but that couldn't be in a novel.

She'll never squeal laughing, she'd never
not bite him, she hates cute girls, she hates
boys who like them. Biting is embarrassing
and wrong & she has no intention of doing it again
but she would if he did if he dared,
and there's no story if there's no hope of change.

THE PROBLEM OF REVOLUTION

On a spring evening late in Lent
she turns 16. The saying she's hated,
"never been kissed," is correct nonetheless;
she likes best a boy she's never dated.

The rose of her dress is ashes of roses,
she's told; & its eloquent silk has quite
a good hand to it. Its self-belt shows, at last,
a waist—though flat not fashionably slight
& round. Her garter-belted stockings
are silk. The garter belt is net & blue.
The cake is strawberry pound, her favorite,
from Dean's. There are fresh strawberries too.
Facing the windows, with mirrors back of her
repeating outside green on the inside view
of presents wrapped & piled, she sits between
the scented aunt who thinks her new
and the cousin, ten, who sees her old.
As she blows out the counted certitude
she turns into still mirror water, cold
at the end of the family table, and comes untrue.

THE PROBLEM OF GRATIFIED DESIRE

If she puts honey in her tea
and praises prudence in the stirring up
she drinks, finally,
a drop of perfect sweetness
hot at the bottom of the cup.

There will be
pleasures more complex than it
(pleasure exchanged were infinite)
but none so cheap
more neat or definite.

THE PROBLEM OF LOVING KINDNESS

She has gone soft
her body suddenly
lovely to her.
Gratefully
she wants to speak & be
believed, to see
his eyes darken with quiet & deepen
learning they agree.
But he believes as if deaf
what he says—
words for shocks of love that sound like
invincible grabs snatches whams hits, like
Cuchulain's *tae bolga*—a weapon that striking
her anywhere would shoot, in an electric
flex of tentacles, need of him
through every member, follicle
of hair, & finger-end—its thousand hooks pointed
so backward & sharp they must be endured
because to remove them would eviscerate.
She has to turn down his talk. She says
if love struck her like that she'd refuse.
If crazed endurance were the only ecstasy
she'd opt for evisceration on the spot.
She feels flat-footed, he's so carried away.
Since he's not listening she's silent;
she eats the rest of what she has to say,
her dreadful dowdy words,
the kind he won't hear,
full of dumb feeling,
"My darling. My dear."

THE PROBLEM OF OUTSIDE IN

Big trees make
the east field dark first. A shadowy
rabbit emerges. Shadowy grasses shake.

The archaic red-gold
that washes far slopes in one gold-red
rims tree-crowns in the west hill-fold.

From their leaves, under-lit
as the sun slips down,
their trunks dangle toward
the blur of ground.

Each such dusk, on the tallest tree top
a robin alights, silent, faces west,
& to the last warm flush presents
its heraldic breast.

She persists as she must, attendant on grace
to say this place into the place she meant,
till she perches as in all real places
on a cliff at the edge of a continent.

THE PROBLEM OF THE DARK

Lacking electric light
or other artifice
the instruction of night
is hit or miss.

Strolling's a dream-state
nightmare to run.
Fields she negotiates
drop to canyon.

She makes her foot wait, feel for
what's next. She's far in.
The edge of the work of her war
is air on skin.

THE PROBLEM OF THE FUTURE

She no longer expects gardens
will have low gates to Eden in them
or in a burst of roses,
flaunt truth from stem to stem

but, because of lovers (who must be
Eve or Adam to what they will see
as the last cement hardens)

the command grows:
to prophesy such gardens.

She prophesies such gardens.

WEARING THE GAZE OF AN ARCHAIC STATUE

The juggler in her suit of nerve
is eyes and hands. The rest of her
dangles soft-shoe below her shoulders,
relaxed, co-operating. She knows
that to toss things out is something
but not much, not important; is
for the sake of when, picturing
a ribboning like water spurting,
she is holding nothing.
She is on her own here;
she is not just letting go,
and her small touching skill is:
holding nothing.

Holding on, she is not a juggler.
She is you and me, hands full of things
she must practice juggling to get out from under.
She sets her feet and begins.
She smiles like Pomona, offering
3, a dozen, lifeless, bits & pieces she
can't get rid of; she presents them as
shapeliness and they lose weight.
The rhythm clarifies something, maybe her.
She settles back, a laughing fountain
pumping particles.
The order of motion emerges.
Up they loft one by one, she is tossing,
up, spheres, sticks, boxes, soft, metallic,
out with them she goes till her hands
close on nothing, are just

touched for the electric
seconds of netting the elements
with energy in air.
They drop, sprout, up, out, drop, up, & slowly
each touch makes her invisible save as
a phase of the great legislation
she proposes to obey.

"LOVE IS NOT LOVE"

...love is not love
Which alters when it alteration findes,
Or bends with the remover to remove.

WILLIAM SHAKESPEARE, SONNET CXVI

"LOVE IS NOT LOVE"

(for Elena Cornaro, first woman PhD, Padua, 1647;
and for those whose children are in pain here and now)

It is cold. I am
drawing my life around me to get warm.
Holes in the blanket can't be re-woven.
Some thorns caught in it still scratch. Some tear.

I reach for comfort
to the left-out lives of women here and gone.
They lend them willingly. They know my need.
They do not hate me for crying. It beats despair.

Elena Cornaro
hands me her cinderella cap & gown.
I put them on. Stiff fur. But intact: she
(when eleven! just in time) saw

in a flash the mortal needles
their rain of cupidity
aimed at eyes across the looking air,

laughed and in singleness averted them
shielded by choice against the dart & steel.
She stopped herself in herself, refined
her will, and brought her mind virgin to bear

stretched across nine languages—nine sun-
keepers, their word-clusters grapes
of intellect, for wine
she pours me now.

It stings like speed:
PhD, TB, breath on fire, young,
she sported her doctoral vair
in vain. She too died of blood.
Yet the mind she trained
had warmed her in the storm
(all storms one storm) where
she'd left no hostage howling to be freed,
no captive mouths to feed;
in her sight, no punctual winter swarm
of guilt—pale bees whose attack breeds
paralysis, and dread of the snow
that masks the snare.
I am stuck in cold. It is deaf. It is eiron.

What has happened to my child
is worse than I can tell you
and I'm ashamed to say
is more than I can bear.

Elena, listen.
My body speaks nine languages but the greed
of me is stuck, my exposed eyes prickle,
I think blank, he's lost out there, I'm scared.

What I have borne, I bear.

Oh I praise your continence, kind life, pure form.
Your way's one way, not mine; you're summer-stopped;
my meadow's mud, turned stone in this icy air.

Whose fault is it? It's at the root my fault.
But in your cape, I come to?
and I'm in your care?
As he is mine, so I am yours to bear
alive. He is still alive. He has not died of it.
Wronged. Wrong.

Regardless love is hard to bear.
It has no hospital.
It is its own fireplace.
All it takes is care.

Well, when you grew intimate with pain,
what did you do. How did you do it. Where.
That, this? Thanks. Suppose I'm not in time,
is it worth a try. I'll try,

try to conceive of room to spare,
a surround of walls steady & steadying
an uncracked ceiling & a quiet floor,
a morning room, a still room
where we'd bring mind to bear upon
our consequences—we who make
no difference, who ignoring
absence of response have chosen
ways to love we can't go back on
and we won't,

regardless:
like your holy aura, Elena,

like your singleness, my fertility,
your tiny eminence, your early death;

like our Vassar Miller, her persistent listening;
like our Tillie Olsen, her persistent flowering;
like our Djuna and our Emily
their insolent beauty visored,
disguised as hermit crabs;
like our Sara Jewett's faithful gaze—
cast down—
like my long-drawn-out mistakes.

Elena maybe we
remember each other as room
for when to cry, what to cry for,
cry to whom.

HANGZHOU, LAKE OF THE POETS

MORNING

Reading the bones, wetting a fingertip
to trace archaic characters, I feel
a breeze of silence flow up past my wrist,
icy. Can I speak here? The bones say I must.
As the first light strikes across the lake, magpies
scream, and the cast bones say the work must come true,
it's been true all along, we are what we do
out on our digs. Dictor and looker, all eyes,
with spade and a jeweler's loupe I sift mud & dust
for bone, for shellcast. Spy, archeologist
of freshness, I expect sight-made-sound to reveal
fear cold at the throat of change, and loosen its grip
so that mind, riding the bloodwarm stream, wells up
as the speech that bears it and is telling.

EVENING

Magpies scream. Though the tongues of birds
say Now and warn forward, free of a live past,
we seek back and forth for change, the ghostly sparkling
of our watertable under everywhere.
If I don't speak to tap & ease it out,
I go dry & dumb & will die wicked.
On the lake of the poets a stone lamp flickers.
It casts eight moons dancing, casting doubt
on the moon that rides above the winter air.

Ice thaws in a poet's throat; the springing
truth is fresh. It wakes taste. The taste lasts.
Language floods the mud; mind makes a cast of words;
it precipitates, mercurial, like T'ang discourse
riding the tidal constant of its source.

LEVELS

A stone fence holds the heat.
Close to it, the earth face opens:
a little eye
rimmed with dirt crumbs;
a nerve inside winks
alive with ants.
The yellow-shafted flicker
before it strikes inspects
the spot, drops
from the fence, calculates,
lifts the lid off.
Air fractures, and
inner alleys collapse, as
diamond-cutter the flicker
like a good writer starts
at the heart.
Its bill its tool,
it chisels toward the fault,
beaks at the crux of it, and
chambers of egg-cases
crack open. As the bird
eats, insects by hundreds
scatter in patterns carrying
clustered eggs, rushing
some to safety, later.

Ants leave me cold,
their bitty parts reflexive,
like cells of lung or muscle,
unprincipled, lacking

a visible body to serve—
oh, why qualify. Ant-mystery
drifts out of mind.
The bird is flicker;
its action exhibits it,
pinioned to a wheel which
the mind's eye axles,
the mind's eye spins.

THE ROYAL GATE

Little Jacqueline Pascal played with Blaise
re-inventing Euclid (Papa told them to).
While he made up conic sections, she wrote plays
& got papa out of jail when Richelieu
liked her long impromptu poem in his praise.
I haven't read her verse. It's not in print.
Blaise invented: the wristwatch, a kind
of computer, fluid mechanics, the hint
for digital calques, probabilities,
the syringe, space as vacuum, the claims of lay
theologians. He thought (he thought) at his ease.

In her convent Jacqueline kept the rules.
On or under every desert there are pools.

OUTSIDE THE FERTILE CRESCENT

Too long out of her seashell, too far away
from green waves sparkling as they lick the sky,
Aphrodite falters. Shallow ponds delay
her sea-search. Off course, inland, tired, dry,
she takes a man's words seriously
when he offers water. He owns a well.
She settles in his oasis. His one tree,
his human heart, cast their spell;
for such implosion she serves him gratefully.
He keeps her safe from his city of those
who are wicked. She gets water enough,
cupfuls, pitcherfuls, to cook & wash clothes,
not to plunge in. Pillared when she calls his bluff,
at dawn her salt crystals gleam, flushed with rose.

DREAM OF TOO LATE
(for Léon King)

I come to tall, with a
shock in my banquet-hall,
two-dimensional this time.
As the crux of the decor I'm
honored, though woven flat & hung bold & high.
Every-colored, slightly rippling, I
supervise, magnificent, a tapestry
worthy, one of Nine Queens all praise readily.
My crown in gold thread forgives my face.
Too late I see how I earned this pride of place.

Too bad. I want to start over, to be
brief, a briefest agent of tranquillity.
I'd be willing to be lily, to grow
set out in April in a tub below
the south casement where under stroke of sun,
lilium, I'd slowly, candidatum,
open my bells, one by shining one.
I would not mind how soon such work is done.
I'd be animal, bird, vegetable,
anything as useful as delible,
the opposite of icon. I wanted me
as easy to alter as air, subtly
tranquil
   like her, there, the younger
sister the harper
makes up a poem for, which he as is proper
does not sing until after his astute
praises of host and hostess. She causes no stir
as she ascends his wit.

She takes her lute
(a page brings it, gilt, small, three strings).
She pushes back her hair and sings,
and—though no one can hear her
since she is only the younger—
instantly everyone's cup is clean, bright, full
of a supreme wine,
its ripe light still.

PLOT SUMMARY

Time threads the random in the order of thought.
The basic survey course (*Gawain* to Milton;
Dryden to Yeats) spreads a net where, once caught,
Webster leads a reader strand by strand to Donne.
Memory weaves a long life's small events
to a tissue of intelligible days.
Some pique the whole length with a figured suspense;
some vanish. The whole plot whole cloth displays
gives time consequence (I met him, then her;
we read Joyce out loud; I had a black silk dress.)
The past persuades me to trust the calendar
and I do—unless I sleep or unless
some wind, some scent like the Hudson low-tide stink
splits time & I think *you*, and *you* are all I think.

SYNTHESIS

Elemental as weather this love
is of delicate appetite.

Leaves must reflect to the air
the surfeit of light they eat.

You are tender as lettuce;
your mineral bitterness is
suspended in sweet water,
my health in its element.

SPRING SONG

Many May nights I've longed, and failed, to see
the singular mating-flight of the woodcock, whistling
up like a moon-target arrow, warbling loud but voiceless,
song shedding fibrous from the instrumental self,
wings slip-streaming a firm sound as they soar.
With luck, I dream of the body of song I've read of
& sometimes sat up, well placed, waiting for.
November, & I wake moon-laved, too late
for the display a woodcock makes—so extreme
that for once in the work of species for their genes
once is enough. May is behind us, that light.
Here are two solid bodies, wingless, bodies of friends
who are never lovers, bare of former wife and
former husband and usual circumstance.
We are two bony poets horizontal under
the wash of moon, its ennobling shadows.
Both love the display of structure,
the service of skeleton; coherence,
our stock in trade, supports the fleshly molding
of years and acts recorded as musculature.
Our lesson is: that our words embody our purposes.
These are decent mattresses
& the space between them wide enough to hold
what we do not need as friends, what lies outside
the writ of our small parliament for good.
Free to dream we do not haunt each other.
What I say when I talk in my sleep
I trust you with, so you may guess that across
my inner sky (as yours, I'd say)
the vertical longing soars.

We leave each other safe. I leave to dream
wings and wing-arms, wristed, hauling
the dark form, its bones full of air, in a surge
in a tube of whistling in a triumph otherwise
silent in unguessable flight, almost
making out in translation
the words of the celebrant
and the syllable it celebrates.

We are too early for the May that elsewhere
lies ahead, locked in its promises,
its power to invent: self as instrument.

DE-FUSING THE USUAL CRIMINAL METAPHORS

Pity the idle who (though daily our lives
must make room for those who use clubs guns knives)
speak as if a penis were, when erect,
a tower of hard. The dear part we inspect
is always quick to shrink from violence;
hand-small, it fits any woman well.
Jocktalk of huge dongs grown trenchant as they swell
stands in, to hide the gathered evidence
of our true brute force; it is greed, not sex,
that we secrete & feed, till it infects
the whole life not the part with rape-like impotence.

The part comes on hopeful, nudging, nuzzling, tip
bent damp and rosy toward a soft eclipse.
Here's no jackhammer jammed home ruthlessly
but the yielding press of stamen under bee,
glowing at the sweetness of us; neatly met
and heedful (clumsy) as we sweat.
Here's no plow, ramrod, sword; no piercing cut—
if root, tender, a root-bud, just unshut;
though worm a word of yes and asking blessing,
though hole a blessing asking mouth of yes,
as one soft-tissued muscle noses plumply through
other muscles, their lax loop drawn. Here, we two
make touch our second sight as, no longer blind,
we each bring a self—big bones, guts, thoughts, hearts—
to local focus, trusting the ease we find
beyond discovery of our nervous secret parts

(as if hot trust might disinfect our minds
and its oils ease the human kind in us
to be in public as in private generous
with exchanges larger than the ease we're thinking of;
as if what we have to make in making love is love).

JAMAICA WILD LIFE CENTER, QUEENS, NY

On a south wind the sea air off
the flats and inlets of Jamaica Bay
mirrors as they do,
almost wavelessly, space recast as
flatness, long
diminishings of blue
borne lightly in toward
earth colors, steel-lit ochres,
rose-mucky brown, greens.

I am a window that takes this in
like a door, or mouth.
I spit nothing out.
I wait—like the egrets,
egrets spread on distant trees
like a wash of table-linen
for the sun to dry.

Were I a room I'd be stuffed
but what windows admit
I transfigure
to the bite-sized images
intelligence eats & eats
eagerly.

Splotches of white
contract, lift
into springing figures; bird.
One by one, one is a leader, up
off the green dark

they go into sun.
They are coming this way
to lunch in the shallows.
I too am good at hunger;
it never deserts me.
I admit as I am able
frank delight
in the deaths and decisions
of visible appetite.
Deep delight;
it is for—not of—myself,
it is for you
I write
of the storage and freshness
of keepers
of the life
of appetite.

THE IDES OF MAY
(for my children entering parenthood)

Every seventh second the wood-thrush
speaks its loose curve until in ten minutes
the thicket it lives in is bounded
by the brand of its sound.

Every twenty-eight days the leisurely
moon diagrams the light way, east to west,
to describe mathematics and keep us unstuck
on our arched ground.

Every generation the child hurries out of childhood head bared to the face-making blaze
of bliss and distress, giving a stranger power to
enter, wound, astound.

BETWEEN
(for my daughter)

Composed in a shine of laughing, Monique brings in sacks
of groceries, unloads them, straightens, and stretches her back.

The child was a girl, the girl is a woman; the shift
is subtle and absolute, worn like a gift.

The woman, once girl once child, now is deft in her ease,
is door to the forum, is cutter of keys.

In space that her torque and lift have prefigured and set free
between her mother and her child the woman stands
having emptied her hands.

HARD-SHELL CLAMS

When it was too late for him to provide
his own share in my happy childhood, my
father stopped clowning out stories & tried
for a whole day to see me—a good try
by both of us. Back we went to the seaside
of old summers, we two, we talked, we swam,
sleek with cocoa butter that caught the sand—
a glitter like chain mail guarding who I am
from his used blue gaze that stared to understand.
Closed, stuck closed, I watched us—far me far him—
go small, smaller, further, father, joy dim
in beach light. Our last chance, last perfect day.

We laughed. We ate four dozen hard-shell clams.
We swallowed what I would not let us say.

OUT OF EDEN

Under the May rain over the dug grave
my mother is given canticles and I who believe
in everything watch flowers stiffen to new bloom.

Behind us the rented car fabricates a cave.
My mother nods: Is he? He is. But, is? Nods.
Angels shoo witches from this American tomb.

The nod teaches me. It is something I can save.
He left days ago. We, so that we too may leave,
install his old belongings in a bizarre new room.
I want to kneel indignantly anywhere and rave.

      Well, God help us, now my father's will is God's.
      At games and naming he beat Adam. He loved his Eve.
      I knew him and his wicked tongue. What he had, he gave.

I do not know where to go to do it, but I grieve.

PATIENT

The woman sleeps, old hand under old cheek,
skin like white iris crumpled, baby-sweet.
She'd let herself go but she's too weak
to organize admission of defeat.
Morning. Her girl tries to get her to speak
but she's too busy with plans to protect
the one thing she doesn't dare lose, her own,
her married name, "i", not "e", that's correct,
not her first name, her whole name, hers alone
(first names can be anybody's). Some days
she can't say it so she writes it. They
steal her name. Eyes shut, she stares at warm haze.
Then she smiles as she remembers to pray:
Trust. Someone to talk to. Something to say.

MUSEUM OUT OF MIND

Whatever it was I used to call you out loud
when I was twenty, ten, or less, I forget. Odd—
I shy from recalling the syllables of how

the golden age once spoke (say, as we talked non-stop
after school, or having our hair done, or as you
chose green peas pod by pod while I watched you shop).

Later, myself mother, I called you the motherdear
no child of mine would use—but one of the baby
humwords must have come first. And I am infant here

before your advanced degrees in death, seeking speech
in words of a tongue I am spelling out of you who could,
by the stars and letters of a map you'd make, teach

(Queens Hermes, alphabet giver) anyone to find
the essential simple, and to translate all
locations into constellations of the mind.

I talk to your absence. Daft. Grotesque. I begin
to see you as grotesque, yes a joke, a guess,
a grotesque of the grave I wept to leave you in.

Birds love dead trees. They like to strip a shred of bark,
tug at it, shake it, lunch on eggcase and insect,
and I go after you like that. Graves are

grounded in the mind though the cemetery keeps
grounds & groundplan, their care perpetual; yours is
in the sad best section, comical—we Stoics

are all comics—among Mafia and their daily,
like you, communicant women. A solitary,
motherdear, you loved the look of community

as, dogged in practise, you believed undaunted
and behaved, relentlessly, as you believed,
so that at times your present company haunts me

like a storm of comic joy. Into the eight-body
plot grandma bought and put grandpa at the bottom,
she went next old raceme dry tiger lily;

then her son and then your man; there you now lie
kept from your father and mother by a layer
of brother and lover   and also by

the costumes, wood bronze lead satin silk & wool,
you each wear. Now you, famous for the Saturday
museum-hauls of your New York, ignore the full

shelves of the Costume Museum Out of Mind
you have entered. Once your heels & skirtshapes looked to
Paris; now you notice none of the well-defined

custom samples, filed as fashion and history;
beaded dresses, bow ties, hard collars, French chalk,
corsets, false cuffs, union suits, hand embroideries,

and decades of dressed hair, an outgrown show of styles,
some rotted, some stained; yet in your choice place are stored
shapes & modes that amply record our tribal

49

grasp of the honor of family, the dignity
of ritual, the self of death. There is not much
nourishment in this but I beak it out. Better be

choking down images of the set greywebbed hair
cocoon your skull is wearing and the tumbled nest
of cowlick at your nape, than to grimace and bear

as I bear the packet I found in your drawer, kept
hidden for sixty years but kept: the lissome, fresh,
bright chestnut yard of hair you cut

to enter the nineteen twenties. Dismay, dismay,
disgusting, it's beautiful, funny, it's yours, mama,
still in tissue paper, boxed, as I throw it away.

CALL

Child like a candelabra at the head
of my bed, wake in me & watch me as
I sleep; maintain your childlife undistracted
where, at the borders of its light, it has
such dulcet limits it becomes the dark.
Maintain against my hungry selfishness
your simple gaze where fear has left no mark.

Today my dead mother to my distress
said on the dreamphone, "Marie, I'll come read
to you," hung up, & in her usual dress
came & stood here. Cold—though I know I need
her true message—I faced her with tenderness
& said, "This isn't right," & she agreed.

Child, watched by your deeper sleep, I may yet say yes.

FRIDAY MARKET

(from Vence, for Mary Denver Candee, 1867–1940)

Under the arch, its ruined walls re-used
as the house-stone of small piles of rooms
(one window each & that spilling flowers)
we enter Old City shadow
on weekly market day.
Tourists, we gossip,
amble, and inspect: handmade candles, sox;
a table strewn with herbs tied in bundles
by grasses, where a child learns her numbers
as her mother makes change; down the street,
leaf-wrapped goat-cheese local as radishes; and
a rosy person selling confections.
I want some. "I make them myself, at my house,"
she says, "of good ingredients."
We buy finger-long beige biscuits, fragrant,
seeded, very tasty, a sackful.
I feel cheerful and grateful.
I eat more than my share.

Days later I wake thinking, "Carroway"—seeds
of such kind sleep as we eat for the sake of descent
to the gone, where I look up safe, years ago.
Mother's mother smiles, shows me a plate of fragrant
carroway cakes, and says, "Take all you want."
I stop crying and do. The seed-bite is telling.
"We have plenty," she says, and I learn
that what she says is true.

MYOPIA MAKES ALL LIGHT SOURCES RADIANT

On the treed slope opposite, vertical
in a close weave of leaves, a giant
woman's face is visible, if
I focus into its shadow-spoken eyes.
. . . it is my face the one
I used to have when in that beauty
all the young own. Its look
is of unripe readiness.

When I put back on my spectacles
it is smiling thoroughly and
is ragged, wrinkled, very old,
its laugh-lines definite,
its softest estimates still
ready to unfold.
It is not symmetrical; one eyebrow
lifts; broad across the forehead
a lock of dark, hair or evergreen,
casts waving shadows.
About the mouth
there is something stricken,
some holm-oak silence facing north.
Winter is coming, giant double-face, old friend.
Winter will replace the persimmon
flagrant at your throat
and the lucky gold fig-tree crown.
To your evergreen mouth only the shape
of your evergreen brow will be
company, as the foliage goes down
flying, worn to the dry fibre,
making its light escape.

EN TRAIN

"Paris in 20 minutes." The old excitement
arrives on time as suburbs flash by,
ugly only to look at, lit, densely well meant.

Non-human nature behind us in the dark, I am shy
with longing. We switch to the rings of human intent.
I prepare myself with caution like a quick reply.

City twin to my scarred city on my continent,
Paris gleams, catacombed with greed. Its stained sky
rosy as with deity at midnight is my light tent.

Live sounds, ground small, pulse from it to electrify
roads that join cities into circuits of consent.
Geography is personal, a map whereby

every journey maps home ground. Confident
we're earth-borne, we can't get lost. I enter the event.

IN ABEYANCE

The day of the transit of raptors
happens every September along
the Hudson airlane or updraft;
bird-watchers set a month's mind for it.
No joiner, I'd never joined them
but today from dawn to twelve
high on Hook Mountain I took among friends
with windbreakers cameras binoculars
a watch at a station between fake owls
hoisted on posts facing north & west
to lure the sharp-shins in.
We had the luck to watch
over a hundred (a Cooper's, two marsh, a kettle
of fifty beyond the Tappan Zee); we spent
hours of disembodiment, selves tossed out to vision,
angels in our abeyance, taking gift as title. Tired,
I cased the glasses, ate apples & sandwiches,
lay supine on warm noon rock out of the wind
to magnify sleep with praises of lenses

and woke gasping at shouting, It can't be! It was,
was fluency, inverse above us for hours,
a river swimming with flying a mile deep
among the invisible: all otherness:
            affluence: as twelve thousand
hawks went over, broad-winged
(an eagle among them, osprey also)
the one species mostly; I saw them,
their undulance communal, some
dropping awhile a quarter-mile afloat

then pulsing up again deep.
                              Hawks
splash difference on the visible the
virtual the not-so sky,
displaying the shaping of air
as they plunge up, into out-of-touch, or
as aloft they liquidly
maintain their openness
fully extended to a rest
that rides deeper in the cells
than sleep or than most desire gratified.
There they take their distance
and a stillness to see it in
that I will die knowing nothing inward of.

They know one thing: when.
Days dangle for them, dipping
down & up, then dip less & less
& slow, till left sun & right storm
halt at a balance, & ten thousand
high nests empty as all leap
forward southward from & to
the when of equilibrium.

Together they ebb from us, emigrant,
their perspective on or in
the now of air, transfiguring.

INSIDE OUT

Dawning on me calmly,
suffused with old rose, while
past the full, just, the cool moon
sinks through dolphin-grey
clouds going beige into morning,
into much more sun,

restlessness
begins to lift the mists
I have in mind, winds
variable, gusts of change.

Alert & quickening, like olive leaves
flickering, grey side, green side,
                   like a school of minnows
darting in shallows over their shadows,
                   like blackbirds at sunrise
their particles of whistles sped sliding
over local surfaces outward to space,

I walk into harvest looking
for its true seeds its flesh-concealed
answers and prophecies—
autumn in a climate so far
mild; migration weather.

PRESENT

Even out of doors there are doors to open.
The deep wild-scape, while they are shut, remains
as urban as TV and two-dimensional
as maps of space- or underwater-traffic lanes.

Portal to my tame attention,
wild beings gleam. A strangeness,
death-racing, gorgeous, goes
about their unknown business.

> The butterfly, fecund, its thousand of
> flown miles aimed for where there is milkweed,
> lights down; it closes its black-netted goldleaf
> camouflage over; opens; closes. Opens.
>
> The hawk makes its passes. Over the clearing
> its shadow slides, to the terror
> of mole & rockdove; jays scream blue warning.
> It abandons its soundless flight,
> drops, strikes.
>
> Just the sound of wings—crow clattering,
> fan-zip of chickadees, the hushed drift
> of owlfall—strikes, startles.
>
> Under oak, arbutus that
> gives its scent keeps its secret.
> Though it announce nothing, the shimmer
> at its edges warns: sweet life.
> > Found and in hand,
> the tree toad is all one pulse.

Though I learn about attention
and the sift of its waiting,
what trapped moments most show are further
doors shut beyond snatches, glimpses;
yet such presence ushers me, to where
though chances of being called do not increase
there is more chance of being present for the choice,
in the rush of Here I am that awe unlooses
with the gasp at unguessed difference.

ANALEMMATIC

Shadows matter.
Here in the country of the sun
the shadow of my body measures time.

"Bonnet De Villario struxit."
On a level in Vienne-on-Rhone
his gnomon takes his time.

I as hour-hand and observer of it
put my light-lack on a line
across the stone wheel-track of time.

Outside the squad of the Zodiac, feet joined,
I point my handshape at the spin
of rounders skipping to celestial time

and observe, I am engaged in day-praise:

Accept, Interrupted Light, this short dark of mine
personal and visible on account of time.

TAKE TIME,
TAKE PLACE

TAKE TIME, TAKE PLACE

I

There lay Lyonesse, a land now drowned.
There Iseult & Tristan acted, addicted
to love as catapult & drug of destiny.
There, beside themselves, they inflected
the story that shapes us, love misshapen
as fate, its gaunt greed beautiful.
Castle cave & philtre worn to sand & less,
legend washes up in the waters I drink
when, tired of walking free,
I long to abdicate to Lyonesse
in drunken fantasy:

      Our clean hotel room is sun warmed. As you
      close with me we sink & sink till we
      rise under each other borne over
      in the lifting falling lift
      of a slow tide quickening
      We plunge where joy is, on a leash of air,
      and resurface in a double
      ruffle of water; our joy crests
      as gasping shaky we draw separate breaths.
      Sea-water fills our cells
      while our doubling selves
      are kept apart by soul & skin.

      As we dress we glimpse from the windows
      the low-tide sea snarl, sunstruck above
      where we may never walk among
      the shadowshapes of fatal urgency,

for it is sunken, sunken,
that honey-suckle land,
its fort rings skyless, nothing left
but seven stones standing and they
under water at high tide.
It is lost, the desirable paradise
   where love greedy as dreams is fatal & excused,
lost, and the road to it
lost, and its amorous acts
pickled in brine.

Sleep take it. Awake I like a drier wine.

Though under the wish to sluice off
wounds and the memory of wounds
I dream I dive hand in hand
with both Iseults, wordlessly
learning to live breathless their doomed way,
in fact even in that dark I feel a stricter lift
of longing for times of choice in the light of day

where I'd say many things to you but never
   lie and say, "I couldn't help myself;"

where I'd have good dreams clear of doom & mystery
   and learn in from out, responsible as ecstasy;
where I might take time, take place, mind memory.

I I

Time & travel change my mind.
Their implicit courses
make choosing more complex;
I lose the single scope
small choice protects.
All choices are losses—except
for true remembrance which sharpens
blunt intentions into acts,
or for false fantasy
which makes bandages of torn-up facts
to stem the haemorrhage of memory.

The landscape I have left behind
waits for me.
In fantasy, I need not remember it:
If I want, it is weather-free,
its mental climate generous;
I can call in, recklessly,
two moons or suns, calm or storm,
and any company.
Those I'd invite wd come peaceably,
the strong, the witty, but done with dispute—
Launcelot, Elizabeth, Finn,
Dilly Dedalus no longer mute
wd join my old friends, first love, lost kin
all looking as I'd wish they'd be,
at ease as hero & heroine.

Effortlessly helpful
like a southern slope, the people
at timeless picnics can praise a sky
clear without their hope;
they can agree about the food, real cream,
trees of sunwarm fruit, good bread;
They are the people I need
as much as solitude;
they'd all smile, according to this scheme,
not disliking me, not dead,
lost, or dischronous, but well met
and interviewed.

These haunts of wish are falsely true.

Real dream-work builds a windbreak
for retrieval & repair.
But I abuse it when I sleep awake,
to hide from grief I will not bear,
in its shadow-acclimated air.
It is rich, such nowhere.

III

Fantasies dampen the pang of cherishing
goods and chances lost or left behind.
I do no work; they can bring back everything
in waves of picture-music, filmy, soft-spined:
melons can bulge above thin greens of spring
as snowmelt swamps the brookbank to scare
big August moths while yes the applerind
reddens in flowering orchards, near where
live & dead share breakfast and at last find
intimate approval easy, in air
which such reverie, obliterating
absence, swindles to vision I can bear
since nothing is asked of me. Day dreaming
reforms loss till it is neither here nor there.

Loss reformed till it is neither here nor there
is double loss. Then let the absent shout
and shake pain's shameful scent on the air—
that will shock the old fact-faces out:
dank spring panic, my fate-embracing stare,
your rage, mine. Let the early dead speak again,
this time to untell the lies death left in doubt;
let their harsh loss start my resurrection
in the plural truth they were and are about.
Though the dead have sealed their eyes and **arguments**
and seasons irk or please us unaware,
marked in the far hawk and the daily wren
the great co-ordinates, perfectly fair,
might haul this place now up through that place then.

This place now—if hauled through that place then
whose salt inner seas lighten my real weight—
beaches my self in my shape, dries my skin,
& grounds me where I can stand to integrate
the crazy hot-cold climates I have chosen
or been chosen by. Bodies met in dream
that I once by drift-fire took to my embrace
confront me as stroke for stroke I redeem
that flesh with this. Time interpenetrates
the memory: match-flare, full blaze, fading gleam,
morning ash. Waking I see as they were then
the lost, towering, remote, but true, their beam
sentinel. I hear old names true-spoken
in the chuckle of the channeled inner stream.

Down the chuckle of the channeled inner stream
I stare for signs, imagining replies,
& endure in echo the spent grunts & screams,
the true relics of my victims & allies.
I squat & study what they meant to mean
and fail but listen: I've stopped saying yes
to the doom of being what I must despise;
doom is not a self but a game, a guess,
a child's costume—and a deadly disguise
I can just get rid of like an ugly dress.
The hard sun of memory, in wisps of steam,
lifts off the make-up, the splotches of distress,
dries up the marsh-wraith veil of false esteem,
and sets off alarm-clocks sharp as happiness.

They set me off, alarmed at happiness,
to join birds in their sanctuary. A tern flies
tilting to its turns with acute finesse.
I watch it mediate marsh & beach, skies
and ocean, balancing stress & stress,
airlift & gravity, with unminded ease.
Its caught fish flashes, swallowed on the rise.
Its high speed fueled by its discoveries,
it pipe-threads upward as its black beak dries.
Its life embraces its necessities;
this federal parkland is its wilderness.
Such grace. It names the saving world I might seize
but am too locked in time to see: unless
we are what our imagination frees.

To become what my imagination frees
my road turns linear. Summer gardens die
a while, above the ground's certain mysteries;
winter shines & deepens like a sleep; but I
leave Eden joyfully; all cyclic repose
dims the human joy I can't afford to lose,
the causeless joy that hears joy as a reply,
and turns my hand to what's left of my true
experiment in the forward of surprise.
Joy's like luck, imagine that! I can't
lose or win it, mean or wild, off or on my knees.
Joy speaks out. And in. The time-line joy may use
is broken and brightens not as I please
but any instant. Its innocence accrues.

On the instant, its innocence accrues
across the cityscape, real and immense.
Here bird and I are each other's news
alighting centered in the present tense.
Inside out I identify bird clues
framed in sun by my binocular guess;
here its lift of head & tail are evidence
its flash of song confirms; here is steadfastness
in single names for thick experience.
"Wren," I say. "Hawk." "Tern." "Luck." "Love." Wingless
and winged we startle then settle, each a view,
alert & modest in our different dress.
I hear unearned joy pay my human dues
and take this passage for my new address.

Climbing the steps, awake, I wake to sense
how dream-tides shape all shores, their forward press
rich in suspended dissolute continents;
and deep under the seas' collapsing caress
are the porches and bridals of Lyonesse.

A NOTE ABOUT THE AUTHOR

Marie Ponsot was born in New York where she now lives. She
is the translator of thirty-two books, most of them children's
books, from the French, and is the author of two earlier
books of poems, *True Minds*, 1957, and *Admit Impediment*,
1981. She has received many awards, among them the
Eunice Tietjens Prize from *Poetry* magazine, a creative
writing grant from the National Endowment for the Arts,
and the Modern Language Association Shaughnessy Medal.
She teaches in the department of English at Queens College.